Drinking, Driving, and Surviving…

Uncovering the secrets of DUI avoidance

By Parnell Worthington

978-1-4303-0271-1

Copyright 2004

Wild Seed Publishing

Drinking, Driving, and Surviving… Uncovering secrets of DUI avoidance
By Parnell Worthington

Disclaimer: A Word of Caution

This book should not be seen as a "how to" book. It is not intended that any of the information contained in the book to be used for criminal purposes. It is intended purely for academic and entertainment purposes only.

Author's Note: Acronyms DUI, DWI, OWI, OUI

Several acronyms for "drunk driving" are used throughout the book. Several states use different initials to describe drunk driving including: Driving Under the Influence (DUI), Driving While Intoxicated (DWI), Operating While Intoxicated (OWI), and Operating Under the Influence (OUI).

Author's Note: Names and Quotes

Due to the sensitive nature of this subject, the "masters" who have been interviewed for this book have asked for complete anonymity. Therefore, the names have been changed and, in some cases, the interviewee has requested that a nickname be used. The author respects those wishes. The author has also used discretion to alter certain quotes in which certain speech patterns and idioms could be used to identify the master. However, all attempts have been made to ensure that the actual meaning, and the flavor, of the information is consistent with the master's intentions.

Introduction: The War on Drunks

Recent statistics indicate that more than 1.5 million people get arrested each year for drinking and driving. Not all these people are raging, dregs-of-society, boozehounds speeding on the road in some gin-fueled death wish and chasing puppies and babies onto the sidewalks. Some are just casual, social drinkers who were in the wrong place at the wrong time—and without the right information.

They stopped off for a drink after work—maybe ended up having two.

Or the game went into over time, or extra innings, and their drinking went into extra rounds.

Their designated driver designated himself a few extra drinks that evening.

In other cases, they're part of a profession that almost demands the drinking of alcoholic beverages. For instance, for the lucky bastard who's the beer taster for Heineken, a day's work could probably be enough to ring the clown's nose on the breathalyzer. But other jobs require a snort now and then in public, too, people like bar owners, salesmen, rock stars, and even clergy.

In addition, life situations crop up on all but the most reclusive drunken soul's calendar that may not require boozing, but they certainly do encourage it.

Weddings, picnics, wakes, and holiday parties, are just a few examples of these types of booze-ready events. But, they're not the only ones.

For example, as one of the "masters" who was interviewed for this book points out, drinking with the boss can lead to a promotion or a big raise. (If you're not careful, drinking with the boss can also lead to a totally new position—on the unemployment line—but that's for another book.)

In fact, American society has a split personality, one might say a hypocritically split personality, when it comes to drinking. Advertisers flood the market with messages featuring cuddly animals and hot chicks designed to promote drinking. Movies and television programs routinely portray drinking in varying shades of hero worship and comedic disgust. Even the government willingly collects taxes on alcohol and automobiles, on one hand, and then, bemoans the drunk driver, on the other—as if those dots would never be connected. Then, to fight drunk driving, the government stiffens the fines and lowers the criteria on when a person is technically a "drunk driver."

Some people might not have even realized just how low the standards for DWI have been dropped—and how easy it is to get a DWI. After all they don't "drive drunk," they just have a couple beers after work and a glass or two of wine with dinner...

Some people might not have even realized just how low the standards for DWI have been dropped—and how easy it is to get a DWI. After all they don't "drive drunk," they just have a couple beers after work and a glass or two of wine with dinner. However, state legislatures across the country have dropped the blood alcohol content (BAC) level for DWI convictions. In some cases, the BAC has been dropped so low that those "couple of beers" and "a glass or two of wine" are more than enough to win them a free ride to the hospital in a State Police cruiser. By the time they saw the lights flashing in their rear view mirror it was too late.

Whether its ignorance or denial, these higher standards have not seemed to deter most people from enjoying an evening out. In fact, if you add up the numbers of

> ## The Master's Notes
> *Like the samurai and the artist, the master of this art learns that preparation and attention to detail are integral keys to their success.*

arrests per year and note the lack of parking spaces in the lot of your town's busiest bar, there seems to be a disconnect. A lot of people, apparently, are willing to put the fines, the higher insurance costs, the jail time, let alone the embarrassment and ostracization on the line for a good night of partying.

To be sure, some of these folks are just in denial—those flashing lights in the rear view mirror are steadily approaching. With each Friday and Saturday night, each Memorial Day picnic, and each office party, the odds begin to catch up with them. That DWI arrest is just a matter of time.

But not everyone fears getting busted—people who seem to have some type of cop kryptonite when it comes to DWI. They beat the odds with such regularity that it can't be a fluke. These folks are the guys—and gals—perched at the end of the bar, week in, week out. They never seem to worry about DWIs or DUIs, or getting pulled over for driving while intoxicated.

They can drink. They can drive. And they can survive.

This book uncovers some of the strategies, methods, and maneuvers of these people—people who exercise their constitutional right to take a drink but never end up with the scarlet letters "DWI" stitched to their police records. It is based on numerous interviews with men and women who have perfected what they refer to as "the art" of DWI avoidance. Some of the interviewees go as far as considering themselves "masters." They approach their art with as much insight and practice as the samurai attends his sword, or the artist reveres his canvas.

Like the samurai and the artist, the master of this art learns that preparation and attention to detail are integral keys to their success. Keys that allow these masters to drink, drive, and survive.

Chapter 1: Just (Don't) Do It

Almost every master interviewed for this book said that the easiest and most fail-safe strategy they employ to avoid DUI and DWI arrests is to simply not do it. The risks and the forces arrayed against them are too great.

Even though studies indicate that people who use cell phones when they're driving and folks who are DWE (Driving While Elderly), can be just as impaired as a person who has been drinking, society has decided to make the drunk driver the politically-correct enemy of the state dujours. Mengele and rapists get better PR than drunk drivers.

The Master's Checklist:

● **Find a designated driver**

● **Use public transportation**

● **Avoid the hard stuff**

● **Know your limits**

● **Sleep it off**

Masters recognize that every time they can avoid driving away from a party or bar, the immutable laws of probability dictate that there is a corresponding reduction in the odds of a DUI arrest.

Therefore, the master takes the extra step to try to find a safe, ride home—it's not easy, but it's not impossible, either. A few strategies they use are listed below.

Have a designated driver

Designated drivers are worth their weight in Coors Gold, but to find one, especially one who is dependable and responsible, as well as one who is willing to go party-hopping on a regular basis, requires the master to make connections with sober people and lightweights.

One master, Mary C., said she actively cultivates relationships with sober drivers.

"I always pray my friends see the light and end their dance with demon alcohol," Mary C. points out. "So long as they keep those rides coming!"

Mary C., a comely female, is more confident of her designated drivers—all males who seem to appreciate her company.

On the other hand, masters, who are anatomically restricted to use Mary C's "womanly wiles," recognize that designated driver system is not, and never will be 100 percent reliable; all had a tale or two about being let down by a sure ride home.

Use public transportation

Whenever possible the master utilizes taxis, buses, and subways.

This is a major advantage of living—and boozing—in a city. Obviously, putting up with smelly, obnoxious, drunk passengers is a problem for sober public transportation users—but, hey, that's their problem. The fines for disorderly conduct are far less than DUI or DWI, the master reasons.

While a boon for city-dwellers, public transportation—or the lack, thereof—is a setback for drinkers in suburban and rural locales. (In fact, statistics from the *Rural Healthy People 2010*, a project funded with grant support from the Federal Office of Rural Health Policy, indicate that the rate of DUI arrests is significantly higher in non-urban locations.)

> *It's not like I can take a bus from Bob's Big Bar located in the heart of Bumfuck Township," Master "Kevin D." stated. "I gotta better chance of getting a ride by human-abducting space aliens."*

"It's not like I can take a bus from Bob's Big Bar located in the heart of Bumfuck Township," Master "Kevin D." stated. "I gotta better chance of getting a ride by human-abducting space aliens."

Avoid hard time, Avoid the hard stuff

Masters will, at the very least, avoid stiff drinks if there's an outside chance they will need to climb behind the wheel later in the night.

Masters argue that they might have an ability to drive somewhat intoxicated, but none say they can drive totally incapacitated.

"Having a beer buzz is one thing; being rocked out of your gourd is another, Kevin D. said. "Most of the techniques I employ require me to keep some semblance of my wits about me."

Drinking rum, vodka, whiskey, mixed drinks and other harder forms of liquor are dangerous habits if the drinker has no tangible ride home, according to the masters. These drinks have pungent odors that are easy to detect.

"A few minutes in the car will fill the whole vehicle with a tell-tale smell that a cop outside the window—hell, a cop passing by in his cruiser—will pick it up quicker than a bloodhound on the trail," Kevin D. said.

The masters indicate that just a little of the hard stuff will impair a drinker so badly that having a cop pull the driver over is the least of your worries; having a cop pull the driver out of a twisted, metal modern art sculpture that used to be an automobile is a far greater worry.

"No lessons can help someone who's playing 'bumper cars' down the highway," Kevin D. said. "At least, drinkers who hit the hard stuff won't need a ride for long, the ambulance, or the hearse, will be there to pick them up soon enough."

"If you decide to get whiskey drunk and drive home you won't have to worry about who to party with," Kevin D. added. "You'll be partying with a whole new crew… down at the morgue."

Know The Limits

Masters know their limits. And they don't try to test those limits like some kind of teenage dare.

They take account of their body size, their body frame, and their general tolerance level for alcohol when they drink and they don't try to attain any drinking-class hero status. Nor do most masters drink to the point of being totally wiped out, as is the case of most neophyte drinkers.

"You've heard of beer goggles and beer muscles, but there's also such thing as 'beer balls,' " Master Albert P. explained. "When you have beer balls you think can do anything after you've downed a couple brews and get away with it."

Albert P. also believes many among young, male drinkers, are afflicted with what he likes to call "JMS", or Jim Morrison Syndrome.

"They're usually kids who keep track of the amount of alcohol they drink like someone's gonna write a biography or a book on their drinking prowess," he said. "Rock stars drink that much because they have chauffeurs."

If there's a chance that the master will need to drive, he or she will set a steady pace keyed to an idea of the amount of alcohol they can consumer per hour, and still be within the legal range. Masters also give themselves a break in the drinking action well before leaving a bar or party. This one small step can allow the blood-alcohol level to drop and dramatically alter breathalyzer readings, masters reported.

Some masters choose to carry a little breathalyzer device that can give them an estimate of what they would blow, if the worst happens. On the other hand, other masters said that these breathalyzer devices should never be relied on—they risk giving the driver a false sense of security. The readings can be inaccurate, and cops have a tendency to manipulate their own devices, in effect "putting their thumb" on the scale to inflate readings a bit.

Albert P. doesn't totally trust the pocket breathalyzer, indicating they have limited use.

"At the very least, they are a blast to take to a bar and see who is the drunkest," Albert P. said.

Masters also say part of knowing their limits means they must trust feedback from their drinking buddies.

They choose their drinking partners carefully—and unconditionally respect the decision of their drinking partners. When their drinking buddies say they have had too much to drink, the master knows it's time to back off the booze intake.

Sleep it off

Taking a snooze in the car for a couple hours is another simple avoidance tactic, masters suggested; but it is one that comes with risks and certain social drawbacks.

"Believe it or not," Master Harry C. said. "In some social circles the act of passing out in a car in the parking lot of some dive is not looked on very favorably."

In addition, Harry C. said that a person sleeping in a car can make himself or herself the object of police harassment. In some states, a person can be arrested for OWI even if the car is parked safely off the side of the road or in a parking lot. If the person is in the car, and the keys are in the ignition, an OWI can be issued, according to Harry C.

In colder climates, this method poses other problems, including dying of exposure—one of the most ignoble ways to shuffle off the mortal coil, a death reserved for the hobo and the street urchin.

Or as Harry C. put it, "So if you decide to sleep it off in a Minnesota bar parking lot in the middle of January, forget about the antifreeze level in your car; you better make sure you have plenty of antifreeze in your own system."

Chapter 2: Preparing

What if? The last resort

Sometimes, despite the best efforts and the most thorough planning, efforts to avoid drinking and driving don't pan out, masters reported.

Designated drivers can be waylaid—usually trying to *get laid*—and will leave their passengers high and not-so dry.

Some people, especially those in rural or suburban areas, don't have the advantage of public transportation or an on-call taxi service.

Risks of exposure may make sleeping in the car a deadly option.

For other masters, driving while intoxicated proves to be the lesser of two evils. Mary C. related a story on this point.

"I was in school and went to a party with a bunch of frat boys," Mary C. said. "It was at a hunting camp way off campus."

According to Mary C., assured of a ride back to campus, she began to imbibe with gusto, trading brew for brew with a guy who was showing her an undue amount of attention. As the night wore on, though, she began to become suspicious. A few girls were acting strange—not in a drunken, crazy way, but in a drugged, loopy way, she said.

"Call it beer wench intuition," Mary C. said. "But I didn't think some of these guys were on the level."

To test her theory, Mary C. excused herself from the crowd, claiming she had to use the restroom. She carefully closed the door to the bathroom, leaving a crack that would allow her to observe her male drinking "companion."

"As I watched, I swore I saw him take something, a pill or something, out of his pocket and break it over my drink," Mary C. said. "Well, I wasn't going to wait on the lab results. I decided escape was the only option."

Mary C. did worry about driving in her condition.

"I'm not saying it was right. I'm just saying I did what I had to do," Mary C. said. "By the way, a couple of years later, a girl told me she thought one of the guys took advantage of her that night, but she could never prove it.

She had passed out."

"I would have probably blown a .01 or a .015, close or over the legal limit at that time," she said. "But everyone else at the party was just as shredded as I was, or worse, and I was afraid they'd give me a hard time and force me to stay. That could have been deadly."

Mary C. said she grabbed her purse, made some type of incoherent excuse, and got in her car. Terrified that every set of headlights behind her belonged to the cruiser of a state trooper, she eventually made it to a convenience store on the edge of campus. She parked the car and walked to her dorm.

"I'm not saying it was right. I'm just saying I did what I had to do," Mary C. said. "By the way, a couple of years later, a girl told me she thought one of the guys took advantage of her that night, but she could never prove it. She had passed out."

> ### The Master's Facts:
> *While males are overwhelmingly busted for drunk driving charges, female arrests are rising. One stat said that the number of female DUI arrests is* **rapidly** *increasing.*

Mary C. said from that point on, she knew that the DUI club was no longer a "men's only" club. She vowed to be prepared, if there was ever a next time.

Statistics seem to back up Mary C.'s observation. While males are overwhelmingly busted for drunk driving charges, female arrests are rising. One stat said that the number of female DUI arrests is rapidly increasing. For example, according to the DUI Fact Book, in 1990, the number of women arrested in Illinois for DUI had increased 48 percent since 1986. Women comprised 20 percent of DUI arrests, up from 12 percent in 1986.

As Mary C. said, "There aren't just a lot of mad mothers out there; there are a lot of drunk mothers, too."

Now What?

For those people who, like Mary C., find themselves in situations in which all other options are expended, masters indicate that the next step, driving after drinking, is the last resort. It's a step to be taken only when it is absolutely unavoidable and when the necessary precautions and preparations have been met. It's a step that should only be taken when there is a definite route—and a definite goal, usually a home base.

The master typically has prepared months in advance for this scenario—priming for the mission and conceiving the most intelligent strategy possible. The master never lowers his or her guard—no matter how much, or how little, the master had to drink; no matter how close the master is to a home base; no matter how many successful "missions" the master has made.

In the following pages, the masters reveal how they prepare for just this occasion.

Prepping the Ride

Masters agree that the first steps to successful DUI avoidance occur months, if not years, before the official "go" signal has been issued. Indeed, for most masters, this process goes back to the actual purchase of the vehicle.

Since some vehicles are more likely to raise a cop's level of suspicion than others, masters choose a common model with as little decoration as possible—a car that won't stick out on a busy interstate or on a back road to nowhere. Some masters even decide to buy a second car—excruciatingly tailored for this mission.

> ### The Master's Facts:
> *Motorcycle operators made up the highest percentage of drunk driving fatalities. Drivers of light trucks come in second. The only people who should be happy that these types of vehicles are on the road are people in need of an organ donation.*

A number of vehicles can be easily weeded out. Motorcycles and pick-up trucks are probably the poorest choices for drinking and driving and masters avoid them. (Lawn tractors—usually the drunk driving vehicle of choice for country and western singers and inbred hillbillies—are better left in the shed on Friday nights, too.)

According to statistics from the National Highway Traffic Safety Administration (NHTSA), motorcycle operators made up the highest percentage of drunk driving fatalities. Drivers of light trucks come in second. The only people who should be happy that these types of vehicles are on the road are people in need of an organ donation.

These statistics are not lost on local police and state troopers when they profile vehicles during their routine DUI patrols. Masters, therefore, shy away from bikes and pick-ups when they embark on a mission. (For the record, tractor and trailer operators have the lowest percentage of drunk driving accidents, however, none of the masters interviewed have purchased an eighteen-wheeler to take to the bars.)

According to one master, who wishes only to be referred to as "Drunk Tzu," sports cars, muscle cars, and other assorted customized hot rods also make easy targets.

"These vehicles were designed to draw attention and, when your BAC is over .08 percent, they draw attention from sources other than admiring females, namely Smokie," Drunk Tzu pointed out.

> *"These vehicles were designed to draw attention and, when your BAC is over .08 percent, they draw attention from sources other than admiring females, namely Smokie," Drunk Tzu pointed out.*

Just as some flashy vehicle models stick out, so do cars with flashy paint jobs. Bright reds, yellows, oranges and purples are listed as the most provocative to law enforcement personnel.

Flashy cars and hot rods have another disadvantage. They indicate the driver has money—and as the masters detail later—the men and women in blue often see green when an expensive sports car or hot rod comes freewheeling it past their checkpoint.

Finally, cops will obviously remember a provocative vehicle than a car that blends into the scenery.

"Maybe a cop is on her way to another call one Friday night when she spots a red 1971 Vette with a hood scoop and silver flame racing stripes," Drunk Tzu said. "Guess what she's going to do next Saturday night when she sees a red 1971 Vette with a hood scoop and silver racing stripes pass by? There's a good chance she's going to pull that Vette over and test her female cop intuitions."

With these facts in mind, the master avoids this potential threat by choosing a common, nondescript vehicle with a subdued paint scheme. Masters add that four-door cars, synonymous with the innocent, family wagon, are preferable to two-door vehicles.

Clutch Time

When choosing between an automatic or manual transmission, most masters will tell you that there is no contest—clutches are worse.

Clutches can grind.

They can pop.

They can cause the car to drift back.

Masters believe that clutches are, generally, just one more thing to screw up when Johnny Law has his mirrored sunglasses pointing in your direction. Masters agree that automatic transmissions are, therefore, vastly preferable.

Decisions, Decisions

All this information may come as bad news to some guys—especially the ugly guys—and cause them to wonder: How can you pick up a super hot chick in a late-model, tan Chevy Nova?

Masters say the power of choice is their most powerful ally.

"If you believe that you might be drinking and there's a good chance you may have to drive, leave the Mustang at home," Kevin D said. "If you're about to embark purely to satisfy your libido, don't drink. Or drink, drive that fine lady home in your super pimp ride and then let her watch you babble like a baby as the cops haul you in," Kevin D. continued. "Mental pictures can last a lifetime, dude."

"Cops are looking for any reason to pull you over if they even have a hint of suspicion you are driving under the influence," Kevin D. said. "That's why everything on your car—I mean everything—must be in good working order."

Boozin' and the Art of Auto Maintenance

Once masters purchase their vehicles, they keep these cars in the best shape possible and make sure they are properly inspected and documented.

"Cops are looking for any reason to pull you over if they even have a hint of suspicion you are driving under the influence," Kevin D. said. "That's why everything on your car—I mean everything—must be in good working order."

In addition to the annual inspection required by most states, masters make regular (and in some cases weekly) inspections to double-check maintenance red flags that could draw attention to their car.

The Master's Checklist:

The master checks his auto to make sure it is in perfect maintenance...

- **Headlights**

- **Signs of body damage**

- **Correct alignment**

- **Cruise control**

Headlights

Headlights are perhaps the most important feature on the car, according to the masters. Masters indicate that, to the average cop or trooper patrolling on a Friday night, burnt-out lights glow like little spotlights of incrimination.

"Cops will use a burnt-out headlight as the perfect invitation to pull you over and sniff around for a DUI bust," Master Harry C. said. "It's like your car was winking at the law man."

Any defects in lighting are fixed... pronto.

"I've even changed a headlight in an auto part's store parking lot on the way between bars." Harry C. continued. "That's how important I take it."

The master takes equal care to make sure the other lights—back-up lights, tail lights, and turn signals—on the vehicle are working.

As will be pointed out later, it doesn't matter whether one or both headlights are burned out—if they're never turned on.

"One guy, probably the best drunk driver on the road, pulled into a convenience store for a pack of smokes," Harry C. said. "When he pulled out, he forgot to turn on his headlights. Two blocks later the cops got him and slapped a DUI on him. The devil is in the details."

Masters also warn about high beams, which can attract just as much attention from cops as driving around without lights on at all.

"High beams are akin to lighthouse beacons," Drunk Tzu said. "But this time the cops are the moths."

Body Abuse

Masters avoid driving a car that looks as though it is some type of high school auto shop project gone horribly awry.

"Severely abused cars—ones with dents, dings, rust, missing hub cars, and the like—tend to receive more scrutiny for a trooper than your typical pristine family Oldsmabuick," Harry C. said. "Cops figure you're either a bad driver, or a drunk driver."

Keeping Your Cars Aligned

The master makes sure his or her vehicle has been aligned properly and the tires are properly balanced. Since sudden jukes and swerves are telltale signs of a drunk driver, this dance of an out-of-aligned car will attract unwanted partners—namely members of the law enforcement community.

"If your car swerves when you release your grip, or you need to maintain a certain amount of pressure on the steering wheel, you are just giving the cops a reason to pull you over," Mary C. said. "Plus, you're just one lapse away from an accident."

For other, like Drunk Tzu, the defect is simply distracting.

"It's one more thing to take you off the road when you're taking a swig," he said. "Get it off the road and taken care of."

Cruise Control

Better than fuzzy dice, or the backseat DVD player, masters consider cruise control not an option, but an essential. Police are sensitive to how drunks typically drive way over the speed limit—or equally obvious—way under the speed limit.

Cruise control makes sure the master never goes too fast, or too slow, and is especially useful on interstate highways with long straight stretches.

Cruise control can also help the master avoid feeling the pressure of police scrutiny if they're being followed.

"If a cop comes up behind me and I have my cruise control on, I know I'm going at a steady speed," Mary C. said. "I'm going to be able to resist the urge to speed up and slow down like some kind of scared rabbit."

Mary C. adds a word of warning on using cruise control. Some stretches of road are subject to a myriad of speed limits; others are too curvy or require too many stops. And some people, Mary C. added, are just idiots.

"Some idiots set the cruise control on 80 and wonder why they got pulled over," Mary C. said.

Stickerin' It to the Man

Most masters don't allow their cars to be a mobile soapbox detailing their allegiances to certain political beliefs or billboards to express their musical preferences.

Whether conservative or liberal, bumper stickers and decals sporting extreme mottos and offensive gestures are designed to get attention—and that is just what masters want to avoid.

"Join a debating society, if you enjoy the fine art of political persuasion," Mark D. said.

Some bad ideas include pro-drinking slogans (Got Beer?), anti-military (U.S. Out of Everywhere), and hippie-type saying (Think Global, Act Local), and gay pride rainbows.

"You want to especially avoid displaying decals from bands that have a reputation for being anti-law or anti-establishment," Harry J. said. "Although, I don't know, if I were a cop and would see a guy going by with a "Carpenters" bumper sticker, I just might have to bust him and let the dude with the "Linkin Park" sticker slide."

"You want to especially avoid displaying decals from bands that have a reputation for being anti-law or anti-establishment," Harry J. said. "Although, I don't know, if I were a cop and would see a guy going by with a "Carpenters" bumper sticker, I just might have to bust him and let the dude with the "Linkin Park" sticker slide."

Novelty items, such as bottle opener key chains and beer-related paraphernalia, are also problematic, masters indicate.

"I know a kid who has beer caps fastened onto his dash," Harry C. said. "Maybe your buddies think this stuff is cool, and maybe the ladies dig it; but Sheriff Buford T. Law isn't going to think so."

Masters indicate that, besides drawing often unwanted attention and suspicion, these simple stickers and novelty items can complicate matters by creating a less-than-favorable impression with police if they're ever pulled over.

This can hinder an opportunity to "create the bond"—and, as the masters discuss later, this is the most important factor to improving the odds of driving away from a pull-over DUI-free.

Good signs?

There are some decorations that masters endorse.

"Since all cops are American, and most are patriotic, I always put a small, dignified American flag somewhere on my car," Mark D. said.

Since most cops have prior military experience, masters may even add a sticker—or two—promoting their own service record, if they have one. (These can also help the motorist pulled over for speeding.)

"I knew one guy who got off because he had his National Guard uniform in the back seat and he told the cop he was on his way to drill," Master Albert P. said.

"If you served in a famous division or on a certain ship let your bumper inform the officer before he reaches your window," Harry C. stated.

Some people, without military experience, may be tempted to add a bumper sticker claiming military service. This could backfire, according to some masters.

"It's risky if you decide to put a sticker on your car, but don't have any prior military experience," Chuck R. said. "I knew a kid who had a Vietnam Veteran bumper sticker. It would have worked fine, had he not been 8 years old when Saigon fell."

"When he got pulled over, the cop, who just so happened to serve three tours in Vietnam, didn't find his sticker, or the kid's claim to be a Vietnam vet, very amusing," he said. "What the cop did find amusing was the wince and the whimper when he slapped the cuffs on the kid."

"Maybe he thought the kid was Viet Cong," Chuck said with a laugh.

Other military gear can prove useful, as well.

"I knew one guy who got off because he had his National Guard uniform in the back seat and he told the cop he was on his way to drill," Master Albert P. said.

Retired military license plates are exceptionally valuable, according to Albert P.

"P.O.W. license plates are golden," Albert P. said.

Other helpful designations masters feel are safe to be placed on the car include Emergency Medical Technician (EMT), clergy, and firefighter decals. These decals can almost subliminally reinforce a bond with the cop.

"They say to the cop that he and the driver are on the same side," Albert P. said.

F.O.P ... FLOP

Perhaps the biggest farce forced on the bumpers of millions of American motorists is the use of the "Fraternal Order of Police" (F.O.P.) decal. Masters unanimously agree that this does little, if anything, to help the cause of the lead-footed or the beer-brained driver.

To begin with, most police never directly benefit from the Fraternal Order of Police programs. Secondly, this scam, which was probably started by a bunch of traveling salesmen sick of getting speeding tickets at each new town and municipality, has been on the books for so long that most cops are wise to it.

In fact, the Fraternal Order of Police stickers and decals can work contrary to the prime directive of establishing "the bond"—the all-important state of empathy between the driver and the cop. Police are already on to the F.O.P. ruse to such an extent that they may suspect that the driver pasted it on just to throw them off the trail.

"Cops are like everybody else—they don't want to be 'one-upped' or 'had,' " Albert P. said.

Car Interior

If the master lavishes an undue amount of attention to detail on the exterior of the car, his or her focus on the maintenance of the car interior could almost be considered obsessive.

Neat, organized, and fully functional, the master designs his car interior to represent everything that an inebriated mind is not.

After every successful "mission," garbage and debris—and especially any incriminating evidence like beer caps or labels—are cleaned out without delay. The interior is vacuumed regularly.

An air freshener is in constant use, and when the weather permits, the windows are rolled down to allow a fresh breeze in and blow the remaining vestiges of "the High Life" out. As pointed out before, driver's license, insurance papers, registration card—in short, anything that the police may need in the event the master is pulled over—must be on hand and kept well-organized, usually in a specific area for immediate retrieval.

For the more audacious master who actually drinks while he or she drives, the vehicle is carefully modified. These masters outfit their cars with objects that can have dual use.

For instance, a gym bag can be useful to quickly hide the spare empty, or a couple cold ones, should the need arise. More than one master insists on keeping a baby seat in the rear-seat portion of the vehicle.

Masters often find baby seats have multiple uses. A baby seat can make an ideal temporary hiding place for empties—either under a blankey or stuffed under the seat itself. The baby seat also can subtly psychologically disarm a cop.

"Who wants to saddle a financially-strapped middle-class guy with a DUI fine," Albert P. said.

"I just crush the can and stick it either under the seat itself, or wrap it in the blankets," Albert P. said. "Most cops aren't prick enough to check a baby seat. But I'm prick enough to put it there."

A used baby seat can be picked up at a flea market or at a yard sale for a couple bucks, Albert P. said, adding, "It's a great investment if it can save you from one life-altering DUI."

There are setbacks to the baby seat. Just like tooling around in a plain Dodge Neon won't get a guy love from the ladies, having a baby seat isn't the best idea for someone trying to pick up chicks. Male masters believe this is a small price to pay for extra assurance on the road.

> ## The Master's Facts:
> *Cops often use an out-of-date inspection sticker as the perfect excuse to pull over a driver they suspect of driving under the influence.*

Papers in Order

Cops often use an out-of-date inspection sticker as the perfect excuse to pull over a driver they suspect of driving under the influence. Masters can not afford to be either sloppy drunks, or sloppy with their paper work.

If the state or province requires that their vehicle must be inspected and emissions system must be checked, then masters make sure that all proof of maintenance are updated on time.

Likewise, drivers must make sure up-to-date paperwork such as, driver's license, insurance card, registration, and any other document required by the state or province, is on hand and paper clipped together. This packet is then placed in a neat area that is easily accessible.

> ## The Master's Facts:
> *Masters make sure they're dressed and groomed appropriately. Masters report this is not the time to find out how mutton chops and Fu Manchu moustache would look on you.*
>
> *Women should look their best… even a hardcore state trooper can melt at the sight of a hottie.*

The reasons will be discussed in detail later.

Photo ID
The trip to the D.M.V. for photo day may be a hassle; but, like the optimist who sees the beer mug half full, rather than half empty, the master recognizes this photo shoot as an opportunity. A good photo on the

identification card can help make a good impression, in the event a master is ever pulled over.

Masters make sure they're dressed and groomed appropriately. Masters report this is not the time to find out how mutton chops and Fu Manchu moustache would look on you.

"If you're a male, make sure you are clean-cut and clean-shaved before you visit the DMV office," Kevin D. said. "If you're female, a trip to the beautician won't hurt because a good-looking ID card might not just get you off a DUI, it may get you a date with a cop."

"If you look like an outlaw, you're gonna be treated like one," Kevin D. said.

Mary C. agreed with Kevin D.'s assessment of why women should keep up appearances.

"I make myself up like I'm going out on a date when I hit the bars," Mary C. said. "Cause I sure as hell don't want a court date."

Gun Rack Flack

Since most DUI arrests happen to young, white males, masters avoid any stereotypes that might closely resemble this profile.

"You know, nothing said, 'I'm young, white, poor, and drunk' better than a gun rack tacked up in the rear window of an old Chevy truck," Albert P. said. "It's like hanging a DUI invitation in your car."

Guns in a vehicle also make cops more than a little nervous, masters point out.

"They really don't prefer weapons in the hands of the average motorist—it just makes the officer put his guard up which is the reverse of the goal." Albert P. said.

So, unless they're going on safari in the future, most masters leave the gun rack off the vehicle and opt to avoid the threatening gesture.

You There, Music Lover

Next to wheels and an engine, the car stereo is the most common feature of an automobile. However, according to masters, the common car stereo is responsible for an uncommon amount of DUI pullovers.

"The radio is not your friend. If you must listen to the radio or CD, put it on before you leave the parking space," Albert P. said. "And keep it there."

"Most of those people weaving all over the road, aren't doing it because they're so boozed up they're seeing a six-lane highway on a two-lane dirt road,"

Albert P. said. "They're weaving because they're trying to find that Led Zeppelin CD that they were sure was under their seat."

Once the radio or stereo is on, a driver loses concentration when he tries to change the station, or search for a new CD. Under normal—and sober—circumstances, these slight swerves are no big deal. But to a police officer on patrol on a Saturday night, these jerks are the spasm of a driver under the influence—and cause enough to hit the lights.

"The radio is not your friend. If you must listen to the radio or CD, put it on before you leave the parking space," Albert P. said. "And keep it there."

"Hey. If they change your radio station to polka while you're driving, you know what you better do?" Albert P. asked. "You better learn to appreciate the unique song stylings of the Jimmie Sterr band, that's what you better do."

Another problem with listening to the radio or CD player while driving is that fast music often has a peculiar alchemy. If anyone who has ever listened to Metallica can verify, driving to fast music can turn the foot on the accelerator to lead and turn the coffers of the state to gold with the influx of fines, penalties, and court costs.

Arguments over music have caused more than a few driver distractions, other masters point out, and is a good enough reason for a little silent drive. Drivers who insist on cranking their stereos to such volume levels that the bass hums like a low-flying Huey helicopter may not just earn the attention of their peers; they may also grab the attention of various members of the law enforcement community. Masters keep the volume down.

If a stereo is necessary, masters turn the radio on the right station before they even put the car in gear. Or, they put in the CD that they will listen to for the duration of the trip. No exceptions to that rule.

Chapter 3: Prepping the Inner Drunk:

The Physical and Psychological Training for Drinking and Driving

No matter how well the car is chosen, no matter how wholesome looking, no matter how clean and neat, the masters realize that it is ultimately their choices and their actions— coupled with a healthy dose of good luck—that will determine a successful mission. To that end, long before the keys ever reach the ignition, they have prepared themselves both physically and mentally for any and all contingencies.

The Master's Checklist:

The master is aware of the psychological factors before embarking on a "mission."

● **Avoid notoriety**

● **Don't be a shuttle service for your drunk friends**

● **Overconfidence kills**

● **Be aware of the hazards of showing off—often rooted in an inferiority complex**

● **DUI arrests can happen because people are too tired, not too drunk.**

Psychological Preparation

Avoid notoriety.

Masters know that, besides serving as an incredible jinx, bragging about drunk driving exploits and boasting of avoiding DUI traps make them targets of law enforcement. Police are social beings and they are connected to the party scene. In a small town or city, local cops are especially connected to the scene, according to Mark D.

These rantings could easily be passed on to an officer who decides to make it his mission to take a driver down.

"You do this, you've made yourself easy prey, my friend," Mark D. related. "I got pulled over 13 times for DUI and each time I talked my way out of it. I kept bragging about it until the day I found out that one of the friends of my drinking buddy's brother-in-law was a 'statey.' From that point on, there was no more talk about my luck avoiding DUIs, nor was he my drinking buddy anymore."

Philosophies do vary on this point, but in general, exposure to law enforcement should be limited to only positive relationships, if possible. Since, as the masters emphasize again and again, the bond is all important, it is imperative to cultivate friendly connections with the men and women in blue.

Albert P. said he doesn't mind fraternizing with cops and, in fact, believes that these connections saved him on at least one occasion. Albert P. recalled:

"We were coming into town from a Memorial Day picnic. I had a few beers in me and one soakin' in my lap, when we saw the check point."

(Albert P. admits he dropped a few balls this day: first, Memorial Day is a horrible day to take a spin under the influence; second, this checkpoint was a well-known hot spot for cop stakeouts. He should have, at the least, picked another route.)

In any event, Albert pulled up, when he spied an officer in mirrored shades coming his way. Suddenly, the cop went for his holster, yelling, "I'll just shoot the sum bitch right now!"

Shocked, but not losing his cool, Albert started to laugh and yelled back, "God knows I deserve it!"

As the ominous lawman got closer, Albert realized that the officer was a guy who lifted weights at his gym—he helped spot the cop as he benched pressed, as a matter of fact.

Like the Crowned Prince of Ales, Albert was waved through the checkpoint, his heart beating a little faster, his head a little clearer.

Other masters disagree with Albert P.'s assertion that the master should cultivate positive relationships with law officers, stipulating that any connection to a cop increases the risk of DUI.

"A friend of the law is no friend of mine," Mark D. succinctly stated.

In either case, choosing connections or lack of connections must be made with care. Pissing off a cop is never in one's best interest.

The Shuttle Service

Another problem masters have with becoming too famous for DUI avoidance is that this word spreads to unsuccessful drunk drivers and those ride mooches who are more than happy to let someone else take the risks inherent in drinking and driving. Soon, the master is the target of constant pleading from these people, who can't take "no" for an answer.

> *"Look, I don't want to be the resident barroom asshole, and friends are great, but are they gonna pay your fines?" Mark D. asked. "I doubt it."*

For the master, this is a bad thing; not only is it annoying as hell, it's a matter of simple mathematics: the more time on the road, the higher the chances of encountering a cop. Driving people all over God's creation also leads the master into unfamiliar territory—another "no-no."

The master, therefore, refuses to trade his or her odds of landing a DUI for the unrewarding position as head chauffer for their local tavern.

"Look, I don't want to be the resident barroom asshole, and friends are great, but are they gonna pay your fines?" Mark D. asked. "I doubt it."

Over Confidence Complex

The master who has accumulated a series of successful missions runs the risk of allowing confidence boil over to over-confidence. Like a fighter pilot who, after racking up victory after victory, finds himself hot-dogging into the gun sights of the enemy, the master who becomes over-confident can become sloppy, forgetting simple rules and leaving their fate in the hands of the gods of irony.

"Cockiness leads to sloppiness," Mary C. said. "When the odds are as stacked against you as they are, you can never let down your guard."

"Squealing wheels at the corner, dragging to the next stop light, and doing donuts in the tavern parking lot are easy ways to get your ass pulled over for DWI," Kevin D. said. *"If you want to do the cops job for them, go to the academy. You might as well get paid for it."*

Inferiority Complex

Masters tend to have their emotions in check and are well adjusted. Mixing a few drinks with an ego in constant need of attention creates a peculiar monster—one with the heart of Evil Knievel and the motor skills of a mentally-challenged pre-adolescent. Masters avoid driving stunts to impress the ladies, or hot-rodding to show off their new set of wheels.

"Squealing wheels at the corner, dragging to the next stop light, and doing donuts in the tavern parking lot are easy ways to get your ass pulled over for DWI," Kevin D. said. "If you want to do the cops job for them, go to the academy. You might as well get paid for it."

"It may sound like common sense, but a six-armed Hindu goddess couldn't count on her fingers the number of guys I knew who got their DWIs from showing off," Kevin D. said.

Too Tired, Too Bad

Often, drunk drivers are tagged not because they're too loaded; but because they're actually unloaded. Not having the necessary rest, coupled with alcohol's natural effect as a depressant, can lead the body and brain to excuse themselves for nap time at the most inconvenient moments—such as, while motoring down a curvy, country road.

Masters make sure their sleep debt has been paid in full.

Physical Preparations

Like the great choreographer, Bob Fosse, police take sheer delight in expanding the limits of the human form in motion as they devise new roadside sobriety tests. Roadside sobriety tests are little dances designed to amuse

passersby, while testing the concentration, coordination, balance, and motor

skills—or the lack thereof—of the DUI suspect.

Masters try to keep up with the latest editions in these Stupid Drunk

Human Tricks. They then spend some time practicing them—drunk and sober.

These tests include:

One-legged stands—Cops will force the suspects to stand on one leg

until they fall, admit they're drunk out of their minds, or earn an audition to

Cirque D'soleil.

Forward Alphabets— Cops often ask drivers to recite their ABC's. Pricky cops will insist that the recitation can not be "sung," ala Sesame Street. Masters also state that some cops will bristle if the suspect said: x, y AND z. It should just be x,y,z. Who knew cops were so opposed to conjunctions?

> ## The Master's Checklist:
> Stupid human tricks that must be mastered:
>
> ● **One-legged stands**
>
> ● **Alphabet—forward and backward**
>
> ● **Touch the nose**
>
> ● **Walk the line**
>
> ● **Follow the floating pencil**

Backward Alphabets—This

may not sound so hard, but even the most literate master finds reciting the

alphabet from Z-to-A difficult. (One master recounted a story of a DUI suspect who said his ABCs and then walked backwards. While the stunt played out very well for the audience on the Benny Hill show, the trooper didn't find it very funny. Thus a night of revelry came to a quick, decisive end.)

Touch-the-Nose—In this exercise, the hand is extended and brought to the tip of the nose. Sometimes both hands are extended and then brought to the nose. This is almost impossible to do sober—which is exactly why cops use it. Still, muscle memory is the key. Constant repetition of this exercise can help the subject improve their performance—even drunk. It doesn't need to be flawless; it just needs to be convincing.

Walk-the-line—This is a law enforcement version of walk-the-plank, except in this case, if you fall off the curb or white line, the suspect doesn't fall in an ocean full of hungry sharks, he or she fall into a court room full of greedy lawyers. The sharks, at least, have some honor.

Follow the Floating Pencil—Following the floating pencil or light beam is more of an effort to check for jerky eye movements. One master claims that the secret is to look at an imaginary point beyond the pencil, light, or object and follow the movement as smoothly as possible.

No matter how hard they are to learn, or how silly they look while they practice, masters try to achieve some level of proficiency in each stunt, often scheduling a weekly DUI workout session to brush up on these skills.

"If Keith Richards can be as fucked up as he is and still have enough hand-eye coordination to play guitar, I can sure as hell learn to walk one-legged when I'm drunk," Harry D. said.

Harry D. pointed out that it's better to practice these stunts somewhere private.

"They see you staring into space, hoping on one leg, and reciting your ABC's backwards, you won't have to worry about being thrown in jail or int the drunk tank," Harry D. said. "You'll have to worry about being tossed in the funny farm."

(Since police are always inventing fun, new games for drunks, masters remain alert to any new roadside sobriety tests. More on debriefing DUI convicts will follow.)

Cop Games for Drunks

Knowing that the odds of beating roadside sobriety tests are often stacked against them, masters devise games of their own.

For instance, one master keeps a crutch in his car at all times. In the event he is pulled over for suspicion of DUI, the master plans to feign a leg injury which will render the one-legged hop and, possibly, even the dreaded touch-the-nose essentially harmless.

Some masters will even fake speech impediments to beat the backwards ABC test and diminish the cop's ability to detect slurred speech. (Although, this must be done with great care, the master who fails to develop a convincing impediment imitation, may end up angering the cop—not a good thing.)

Also, faking a speech impediment may end up sounding like a lisp, some masters indicate. In this case, the subject may promote negative stereotypes.

"Don't let the Village People fool you," Harry D. said. "Not all cops have homoerotic tendencies."

The Master's Checklist:

Masters know that cops stack the deck against them with sobriety checks. They try to make preparations to fake their way through the tests using:

● **Crutches**

● **Slings and braces**

● **Wheelchairs**

● **Speech impediments**

Chapter 4: Planning

Master Drunk Tzu:

Know your self, but not the cop and you win half of your battles.

Know the cop, and not your drunken self, and you only win half of your battles.

Know the cop and your self, and you shall win all of your battles.

The average road boozer would probably think that by undergoing the preceding preparation and exercises are enough to avoid DUIs—they may even think the constant preparation is overkill.

Not so the master.

Like a professional athlete, preparation means little if there is no plan. Hence, a master studies his opposition, then conceives and studies a series of plans to suit every possible contingency.

In creating a plan, the master first considers the terrain—in other words, the route the mission may take.

"I know exactly what places I'm going to hit and I know the exact route I am going to take home so well that I could drive it in my sleep," Harry D. said, "There's none of this driving around and letting trouble find me."

This master believes in establishing a fairly regular routine, driving over the same road with such regularity that he almost becomes a member of the neighborhood. He drives politely through his route and keeps in good rapport with the residents. (Driving polite is a recurring theme for masters.)

"I wave at them," Harry D. said. "Not like a freaking lunatic, but a casual wave, give 'em a smile, or a polite head nod. I don't speed through their territory. I don't litter. I don't do anything to aggravate them so they never have a reason to pick up that phone and turn me in. They don't have a clue that I'm drinking and I plan on keeping it that way. Hell, they might think I'm part of neighborhood watch."

> *"I know exactly what places I'm going to hit and I know the exact route I am going to take home so well that I could drive it in my sleep," Harry D. said, "There's none of this driving around and letting trouble find me."*

If Harry D. decides to hit a new bar, or is going to a party at a location he is not familiar with, he believes in doing his due diligence beforehand.

First, Harry D. scouts what he calls the "A.O." (area of operations) in advance. Before deciding on the most likely route, he notes any features or factors he considers problematic—such as roads that go through school zones or go past shopping centers or malls.

"Even when schools are not in session, or when stores are closed, they often employ security twenty-four, seven," Harry D. explained. "On slow nights, which are pretty much every night, these rent-a-cops are just dying to get a chance to play grown-up cop."

Be a Good Scout: Scouting Missions

Scouting missions may also uncover police pulling speed trap duty along the route—these sites are often just as handy for Friday night drunk patrols. The master will even note potential hiding sites for cops—roadside pull-offs hidden behind buildings or obstructed by landscape and emergency lanes that connect divided highways are some of the most frequent spots for cop hideouts.

A master also notes areas of high police concentration, such as restaurants and—dare we say—donut shops. One would think that avoiding roads

"A guy I know got busted 200 feet from a state police headquarters," Harry D. recalled. "He was speeding by, high as a kite, and they busted him. Hell, he might as well drove into the parking lot and turned himself in."

that go near police stations would be obvious to include.

"A guy I know got busted 200 feet from a state police headquarters," Harry D. recalled. "He was speeding by, high as a kite, and they busted him. Hell, he might as well drove into the parking lot and turned himself in."

All municipalities, small towns in particular, have traffic pattern quirks that only locals know, Harry D. noted. Scouting missions can prepare the master for these hazards.

"Streets that suddenly become one way, stop signs hidden by low-hanging tree branches, and a billion other idiosyncrasies of traffic can cause the driver to become confused," Harry D. said. "This makes these drivers natural targets of law enforcement."

> ### The Master's Facts:
> *A "wingman" can serve as a navigator and an all-important lookout during road trips to areas unfamiliar to the master.*

Harry D. tries to avoid drinking at in-town pubs and taverns in unfamiliar places. If he must, he employs a wingman, who hopefully has knowledge of the town, or who, at the very least, can serve as a navigator, watching out for signs and unexpected changes in traffic patterns and cops.

Master's know that complacency can spell disaster. Road construction and traffic accidents—especially with all those drunk drivers on the road—can wreak havoc on the best-laid plans. Therefore, masters, like Harry D., reconnoiter several alternate routes if the main road home is no longer viable.

Network

Masters also identify and interview fellow masters about the level of law enforcement involvement.

"When I hit a bar, especially when I hit a new bar, I'll talk to the old guys," Harry D. said. "You know, the old vets and regulars that are usually sitting at the corner of the bar, minding their own business. They can offer volumes of info on who the cops are, when they're on patrol, where they like to hide, their shift changes and things like that."

Harry D. has set up an extensive network of masters and relies heavily on their intelligence. In return, he offers insights in his own area.

De-briefing

Masters are constantly trying to refine their art. To do this, they investigate, and refine their plans based on this new information.

For instance, the master finds the best advice on how drinking and driving is treated in his or her state or locality from people who have been busted for driving under the influence.

These stories aren't hard to find. They regularly appear in your newspaper and on the local television news—usually on Sunday or Monday, after a good weekend binge. Details also spread through local watering holes like spilled beer on a table top.

Masters try to get the information first-hand from these folks.

"You may find some who are reluctant to dish the details, most are more than happy to give you particulars," Albert P. said. "They'll also have a litany of drunkards regrets—a list of 'would'ves and should'ves.' "

According to Albert P., people he interviewed have uncovered the perfect hiding spot that troopers use and times that cops are most likely to be on patrol. They also revealed behaviors and maneuvers that are not successful with law enforcement officials of that particular area. Information was also ascertained on what bars are being targeted for investigation—so-called "nuisance bars," which will be discussed in detail below.

"All that information is gold, man, gold," Albert P. said.

Information from primary sources tends to be more detailed and reliable, masters indicated; however, this is not the only source of data on drunk driving. A regular review of media accounts can give the master inside information. Masters read the local newspapers and watch television to discern patterns of police activities, i.e. when they patrol and where they patrol. Local news radio can also offer up-to-date information on potential trouble spots and areas where exposure to law enforcement personnel may be increased—for instance traffic accidents and road construction.

"I know that there are almost as many cops at a traffic accident as there are at free donut day at Krispy Kreme." Albert P. said. "That's just one more reason that I don't listen to a music station when I'm on a mission."

Another good source of information on cop whereabouts is the handheld scanner, Mark D. said. He carries one with him on most missions— even toting it into a bar on occasion.

Avoid "nuisance bars"

Masters give a wide berth to so-called "nuisance bars." Nuisance bars are taverns and clubs that have gained a reputation—a bad reputation—with members of the law enforcement community. There may be excessive fighting at these places. There may be complaints from neighbors. There may be an undue number of arrests near these places, or a large number of accidents caused by people who have just visited these establishments.

> **The Master's Facts:**
> Nuisance bars are not just nuisances to the people who live within ear-shot of the establishments; they are also a nuisance to the master. Typically these places are under continual surveillance by cops, who use DUI enforcement as a way of hindering patronage of these bars.

These bad reports increase the likelihood that these taverns and the areas around these taverns will receive heightened police scrutiny. In addition, cops use DUI enforcements as a method to disrupt patronage of these "Nuisance Bars."

The master doesn't even drive near nuisance bars, let alone patronize them.

Parking Plan

When possible, masters park their vehicle away from a tavern parking lot and walk the few extra yards. This could mean parking around the corner from their favorite neighborhood pub, or at the other end of the parking lot, if the bar is in a complex with several other businesses.

"My favorite bar shares a (parking) lot with three other businesses, including an all-night grocery store chain," Harry D. said. "I park near the grocery store so that if the police are ever called to the bar, or make a pass nearby, they may not notice my car."

If on-street parking must be utilized, Harry D. said he tries to park in a place that limits the exposure of his license plate, for example, in front of another parked vehicle.

Check point ... Checkmate?

The master is concerned, but not intimidated, by news of DUI check points or roadblocks.

They endeavor to find out likely places of DUI checkpoints. They obtain this information by reading the newspaper: police public service officials love to brag about where they had the check point and what a catch they had that night.

"Where I live, believe it or not, cops like to announce what days they're having their check points," Albert P. said. "I guess they want to scare me. The only thing that scares me is the stupidity of announcing an unannounced checkpoint."

Also, check points tend to occur at regular places at regular times and places—usually on the late nights and early morning of weekends and on prime drinking holidays: Memorial Day and July 4th weekends.

"How many times have you been stopped at a check point going to Sunday school?" Albert P. asked. "Note where these check points occur with any degree of frequency and **AVOID THOSE PLACES.**"

Checkpoints are also preceded by a flood of rumors and innuendoes that can serve as a tip off.

Albert P. is not afraid of checkpoints; quite the contrary, by tying down a group of cops to one point, the tactic opens up more lanes of maneuver.

"The check point should bring a smile to your face," Albert P. said. "It does my heart good to see eight or nine cops in one place and not roving around trying to find me."

"The check point should bring a smile to your face," Albert P. said. "It does my heart good to see eight or nine cops in one place and not roving around trying to find me."

"Plus, I've read that they pull over one out of three drivers," Albert P. said. "I'll take those odds."

No Scenic Detours

It's often easy, masters indicated, to drift off of the main route to do some exploring—some Sunday drunk driving.

That's a dangerous urge, masters agreed. By venturing off the known, proven path, the driver can be mired in any number of unexpected situations and the unexpected is the enemy of the master. Masters resist this urge by driving on the main route, and using alternative roads only when necessary.

Stop the Stops

Masters all concur that making stops—for smokes, eats, and gas—after they have been drinking is a serious mistake.

Besides introducing the master to elements of the unexpected, these excursions also can extend the time the driver is on the road and, thereby, increase the odds of exposure to law enforcement elements. Stops can also increase the likelihood of mistakes, such as the aforementioned headlight forgetfulness.

"I once knew a man who stopped at the ATM for some more drinking money," Drunk Tzu said. "He forgot that he engaged his turn signal upon entering the bank and then pulled back on the highway. The police followed him for two miles, and he never made a right turn. They eventually forced him make a right turn onto the highway berm, where they read him his rights."

Cell Phone from Hell

Also, cops are not the only enemy of the drunk driver. With the advent of the cell phone, the guy on the other side of the pump, the customer in front of the line, and even the kid at the drive-in window, can easily alert the authorities if they see any of the tell-tale signs of drinking.

Before he heads out to a party, the master drives sober to the store to pick up cigarettes, snatch some cash, grab a six pack, buy a couple beef jerkies, fill up his tank, replenishes the old porno supply, or whatever else is desperately needed.

Stopping for food and drink can also increase the number of distractions for the driver. Although they don't hand out "DWM" (Driving While Munching), masters avoid having a bite to eat while on the road.

"You drop your relish dog and you drop your guard," Harry D. said.

Excuses, Excuses

Another good thing to take drinking and driving, masters report, is a well-honed and well thought out excuse, or two, that explains their purpose and destination.

"You'd be amazed of the number of people who answer 'just drinkin' a couple beers,' when the cop asks them what they've been doing," Albert P. said. "All because they don't have a decent excuse."

Albert P. raises the level of excuses to an art form. It may include props—like fishing poles—and certain types of people—like female co-conspirators.

"You'd be amazed of the number of people who answer 'just drinkin' a couple beers,' when the cop asks them what they've been doing," Albert P. said. "All because they don't have a decent excuse."

For instance, on one occasion, when Albert P. was pulled over at 3 a.m., he merely pointed to the fishing rods in the back seat and succinctly explained he was on his way to pick up a buddy to hit the lake. The cop nodded and politely pointed out he had a broken tail light.

Sometimes, Albert P. drives with a child safety seat in the back and a fine young thing up front.

"I choose to drink with women for a variety of reasons," Albert P. said with a smile, "But, one reason is, that if I'm pulled over by the cops, I'm just going to say I'm taking my fiancé to relieve her babysitter."

He hasn't needed to use the excuse yet, but he said he sure enjoys the company while waiting for the opportunity.

Some other excuses the masters use include:

- "I'm on third shift and I just left work."

- "I'm heading to Miami for reunion of old Army buddies and wanted an early start."

- "I'm heading to the hunting camp for a breakfast meeting."

Masters think up their excuses in advance and make sure they are airtight and must be prepared to add specific information that is hard to verify. For instance, in the above example, the master must be prepared to offer information on the name of the factory, the department he or she works in, the hours of the shift, etc. Some cops will pry.

"I'm always aware that the cop could have a relative that works there, so I would say that I just started on the clean-up crew," Drunk Tzu said. "If I would use the Army buddy Florida reunion scam, I'd also have info on what division I was in and what hotel I'd be staying at. I'd be damn sure I was heading toward Florida, too, or at least, have an excuse why I wasn't—like I was on my way to pick up an Army buddy for the trip."

The excuses must also fit the area where the master lives, as well.

"You don't want to say you're on your way to go ice fishing if its July and you live in Louisiana," Drunk Tzu added.

Drunk Tzu pointed out that just as there are good excuses; there are bad excuses. One of the worst, according to Drunk Tzu, and the most over-used is the I-had-a-few-drinks-and-heading-straight-home line.

"Police have heard that so many times, it should be set to music and become the drunk national anthem," Drunk Tzu said.

Checklist

Some masters make a mental (or even written) checklist before they start their vehicle after having a few beers.

Drunk Tzu's checklist is short and simple enough, but indicates it helps him focus on the upcoming mission:

- Turn radio off or turn favorite station/CD.

- Make sure lights are on… and high beams are off.

- Check rearview mirror.

- Double-check that the turn signals are not engaged

(Drunk Tzu frowns on making unnecessary stops, especially on a "night mission." If a stop is absolutely necessary, Drunk Tzu mentally goes through his checklist of preparations all over again before pulling out from the store or bar, making doubly sure that his headlights are on.)

S.O.B. (Six-pack On Board)

Of all the masters interviewed, Drunk Tzu is the most audacious. He doesn't just drink then drive. He likes to drink AND drive. It must be noted, he distances himself from out-of-control, free-wheeling boozers, by limiting this extremely risky behavior to specific occasions and certain consumption limits—such as a beer or two.

"I just like to have a beer on the commute from work," Drunk Tzu claimed.

> ## The Master's Checklist:
> Masters use focus and simplicity before they embark on a mission, often creating task lists.
>
> - **Turn off radio or turn on favorite radio station or CD.**
>
> - **Make sure lights are on... and high beams are off.**
>
> - **Check rearview mirror.**
>
> - **Double check that turn signals are not engaged.**

99 Bottles and Cans on the Floor

According to Drunk Tzu, he only buys beer in cans.

"Bottles are problematic on several counts," Drunk Tzu stated. "For starters, they roll all over the gad damned place and once the cops pull you over, it's a little too late to tidy up and are hard to keep track of. Plus, the noise of those bottles rolling around breaks my concentration, man"

Drunk Tzu said a second reason he avoids bottles is, the rattling can attract attention. He described the sound of loose bottles in a car, as the alcoholic's Jingle Bells.

"If you pull up next to another car in traffic and your windows are open, you risk exposing your mission to some do-gooder with a cell phone," Drunk Tzu said.

In addition, in winter, bottles can explode, Drunk Tzu pointed out.

"Once they explode, cops can not only use their sense of sight and hearing to bust you" Drunk Tzu said, "Now, they can use their sense of smell."

Finally, cans can be crushed to hide easily and minimize detection. Drunk Tzu has a specific way to crush cans to minimize movement and noise. He squeezes the can in the middle, toward the bottom, so the opening of the can points upward. The maneuver also limits the amount of backwash that can leak out, and, accordingly, reduce the smell.

Drunk Tzu said that he keeps no more than three empties, four at the most, in the vehicle at one time. He has modified his vehicle so that these crush cans can be deposited into the trunk by sliding them between the back seats.

"I've also been known to use gym bags to tote freshies and hide empties," Drunk Tzu said.

Drunk Tzu said his first lesson in the importance of disposing empties was profound.

I was waiting for my friend, a singer in a local rock and roll band, at the free clinic—he had, to impolitely put it—a case of the rock star drips that he no doubt, received from one of the many groupies that trailed after his band of hair-moussed gypsies like leather-clad bitches in heat," Drunk Tzu said. "Little did I know that such a small organ could cause such a long wait."

According to Drunk Tzu, he waited in his car for his friend for a few hours when the heat of the summer afternoon proved to be too much for his thirst; and his impatience proved to be too much for his sobriety. He set off in search of a six-pack shop.

Drunk Tzu said he drank five of the six beers as he waited. When his friend came back, he asked his friend to dispose of the empties and the plastic ring, while the last can rested in his lap.

"Almost as soon as we pulled out, a local cop appeared behind us and hit the lights," Drunk Tzu said. "Immediately, my friend, always the good wingman, inquired if he should hide the last beer."

Drunk Tzu told his friend that it would not be necessary. He suspected that someone had observed him drinking the beer and called the cops.

"When the officer appeared he looked at the beer in my lap and asked me if I knew that drinking and driving was a crime," Drunk Tzu said. "I replied that I was familiar with the law and that I could explain."

Drunk Tzu told the cop that he was waiting for his friend and that he was extremely thirsty. Since Drunk Tzu was unfamiliar with the town, he explained to the officer that couldn't find a convenience store; all he could find was a bar down the street from the parking lot.

> ### The Master's Facts:
> The master always disposes of any evidence. The master's vehicle contains certain depositories especially for this purpose or he or she will take every opportunity to throw any cans, bottles, or paraphernalia in the trash.

"I told the cop that I didn't buy a Coke, because I didn't want to look like a queer," Drunk Tzu said. "The officer laughed at that."

"Then I told him I just bought one beer—this one," Drunk Tzu said as he pointed at the can in between my legs. "The officer looked around for any evidence of other cans and when he discovered none, he just asked me to pour out the remaining beer in my can and get out of town."

Drunk Tzu was off the hook.

"If I didn't remove those empties that story would have had a much uglier ending," Drunk Tzu concluded.

As noted before, some masters choose to hide empty cans by, for example, using a baby seat as a hiding place. While Drunk Tzu has never used the baby seat as a hiding place, he believes the practice, in theory, is strong.

It's not just the cans that need to be thrown away, Drunk Tzu pointed out. All evidence must be tossed, he added. Drunk Tzu called the failure to dispose of beer packaging another "rookie mistake."

"Some people just throw those six pack boxes or rings on the floor of the car," Drunk Tzu said. "Bad move. The cop not only knows you been drinking, but he can come up with a pretty good estimate of how much is coursin' through your veins."

"Also if some empties are missing the cop may deduce that you threw them out on the highway," Drunk Tzu continued. "The cop hates the litterbug almost as much as he hates the bar fly and will fine accordingly."

Cool, Cooler Coolest

Drunk Tzu also indicated the cooler-in-the-back-seat is no hiding place.

"But, if you wanna mess with the man, put a cooler in your car, and fill it up with soda," Drunk Tzu said. "This is using deception to gain victory. Very wise."

"Only an idiot rides with a case of beer on the seat. The proper place for a case is always in the trunk," Drunk Tzu added.

Camouflage and Subterfuge

With the popularity of the cell phone, the risk of drinking on the road has increased exponentially. Masters avoid it, and when they do, they use Drunk Tzu's admonition to use ruse and deception to outwit those who would stand in the way.

To begin with, masters carefully camouflage their cans. They'll pour the fluids into a soda can, or put it into a fast food restaurant cup. Wraps, such as the kozees, provide adequate protection, according to some masters.

"If I'm drinking a forty ouncer, a paper bag will occasionally suffice," Harry D. said, noting that some drinkers would scoff at such a limp-wristed ruse. "One guy I knew put vodka in his windshield wiper fluid receptacle and hosed it into his car." Harry D. said. "Now that is extreme."

> *"If you notice, people tend to guzzle their beers," Albert P. said. "This increases the exposure time on the road. A quick hit is the best"*

Masters take quick drinks only on stretches of the road that offer an uninterrupted view of oncoming traffic. Since police can pop out of anywhere, they "keep 'em down" as they approach hills and turns.

"If you notice, people tend to guzzle their beers," Albert P. said. "This increases the exposure time on the road. A quick hit is the best."

Drunk Tzu agreed with Albert P., but said he won't even take a swig at a stop sign, or at a red light, knowing that these areas are under observation by police and nosy members of the do-gooding public.

When possible, masters choose to drive away from the sun to put the eyes of oncoming traffic, including oncoming police traffic. This worked great for planning a route home for Albert P.

"In the summer, oncoming traffic was blinded by the sun," Albert P. said. "I could have waved at the cops if I wanted, but I'm too sharp for that."

He doesn't totally rely on this tactic, he added.

"Of course, if you're gonna insist on that, you discount nearly all east and west travel," Albert P. pointed out.

The eyes are the windows of the soul, some dork poet once said. For the cop, they are the open windows to the guilty conscience. If the master encounters an oncoming cop on the road, the master's eyes are kept on the road.

"I don't make eye contact and risk revealing my blood-shot beanies," Kevin D. said. "I always take a shot of Visine to clear my eyes just as I leave the bar."

Scent Grenade

Kevin D. keeps an unused air freshener, still in its wrapper, hanging in his car. He calls this his "Scent Grenade."

"If I get pulled over, I just rip the thing out of the package and it will instantly flood the car with a powerful aroma," Kevin D. said. "Powerful enough, I hope to cover any traces of the smell of alcohol."

"If the cop complains of the strong scent, I just tell him that my wife just bought the damn thing," Kevin D. said. "He should relate to that. Hopefully, it will be a male cop."

Chapter 5: Timing

Many masters believe that certain days, certain times, and even certain weather conditions are more favorable for a "mission."

At first glance, Drunk Tzu's weather preference seems to be contradictory—contradictory, unless you follow the subtlety of his logic. For example, he prefers bad weather to good, going as far as saying that he favors driving during a snowstorm.

"For one reason, the police are already up to their badges in attending to other accidents," Drunk Tzu said.

"Cops might be hesitant to leave the confines of a nice, warm, and exceedingly dry cruiser to check and see if you're a beer-or-two over the limit," Drunk Tzu said.

Secondly, Drunk Tzu said that if he spins off the road, most cops will attribute it to ice on the road, not to alcohol in the veins.

For similar reasons, rain storms and rainy weather can serve as adequate cover, he said.

"Cops might be hesitant to leave the confines of a nice, warm, and exceedingly dry cruiser to check and see if you're a beer-or-two over the limit," Drunk Tzu said.

Times on Your Side

Masters also believe that some hours are better for a mission and plan to take advantage of those times.

According to Chuck R., the best times to beat the DUI patrols and checkpoints are during the hours when the authorities would least expect you to be on the road.

Morning and early afternoons seem to be the best, Chuck R. said, adding that he learned this lesson from years of factory work.

"I worked third trick. Sometimes we would hit the bars after work for a round." Chuck R. said. "In thirteen years of after-work specials, I have never seen a cop… never."

He also added that he undertook an informal study at his workplace. Many workers who achieved permanent first-trick status, achieved their first DUIs soon after, his study seemed to indicate. On his third-trick crew, there was only one person arrested for DUI; the morning shift had five.

Last Call for Alcohol, First Call for a Lawyer

If masters do venture out during normal drunk driving hours—between 5 p.m. and 2 a.m.—they do so with great care, and with an attentive eye poised to the clock.

"The time you decide to hit the road is critical," Drunk Tzu said.

Waiting until the bar is closing is way too late, according to Drunk Tzu, and last call isn't much better.

"As last call approaches, cops start circling the parking lots of hot spots like a great white shark, called in by the chum of stale Bud and the thrashing of a mass exodus of drunks struggling to exit the premises." Drunk Tzu poetically said. "Leave before the bar closes."

> **The Master's Facts:**
> Cops prowl parking lots of bars and taverns as closing time approaches. (That time varies from state-to-state and from city-to-city, but cops are aware of it!) Most masters leave the bar an hour or so before last call.

He advises those who want to avoid drunk drivers to stay off the roads during these times.

"These are times when the truly messed up are on the road," Drunk Tzu said. "Actually I should say all over the road."

Drunk Tzu leaves an hour before last call. About the time he is ready to leave, Drunk Tzu begins to watch the door. He leaves a few minutes after someone—preferably someone going in his direction—exits. Or, alternately, he'll wait in the parking lot for someone to exit the premises and is heading in his direction. Then, he'll follow that person a minute or two later.

According to Drunk Tzu, this person will encounter law enforcement before you, especially if the cops have the bar under surveillance.

"He, or she, is your worthy pathfinder and a possible lightning rod for law enforcement," Drunk Tzu said.

Happy Holi-DUI!

Drinking and holidays just go together, don't they?

You bet they do, masters reported, indicating that the cops know they do, too. That's why more cops are patrolling the streets and staffing checkpoints on holidays.

Bah Scumbag!

"Worse, cops aren't in particularly good moods during the holidays, either," Kevin D. said "After all, you're the jerk whose making them work on a holiday."

> *"Worse, cops aren't in particularly good moods during the holidays, either," Kevin D. said. "After all, you're the jerk whose making them work on a holiday."*

Some holidays are worse than others, he indicates. While Christmas and New Years get a bad rap, Kevin D. said that Memorial Day and July 4th are the worst possible days to be out on the roads—drunk or sober.

"New Year's Eve is a picnic compared to the summer holidays," Kevin D. said. "Some cops are even filled with the holiday spirit during Christmas or New Years, but on Independence Day, they're out to earn their pay."

Chapter 6: Know Your Wingman

As mentioned in chapter three, the master is not only stingy about taking on passengers, but is also picky when choosing just who is lucky enough to score a ride with the master.

The master does not run a shuttle service—each minute more, each mile extra he or she must drive is one minute, one extra mile closer to be spotted by a cop. Also, with the overwhelming number of statistics on their side, cops are on the lookout for groups of young males.

"The only time you should travel with a whole pack of your young white homies squashed in a little vehicle on a Friday night is when you decide to audition for 'Cops.'" Drunk Tzu said. "For the law, two guys riding in a car is normal; four males is a party," Drunk Tzu said.

However, Mary C. pointed out that any large group of people in a car, even if they are all female, will draw the unwanted attention of law enforcement personnel.

A master, therefore, will only offer rides to one person—two people at the max. And these people will be closely scrutinized and meet certain requirements.

"You can't imagine the people who get busted because their passenger was hanging out the window like a freaking idiot, or flipping someone off," Drunk Tzu said, "One chick I knew got her DUI when her friend flipped off a cop!"

Masters choose to avoid people who are apt to start trouble. They insist on driving with people who aren't prone to flip off cops, moon pedestrians and passing motorists, hood surf, yell, rubber-neck, and, in short, act like an asshole.

Drunk Tzu said knowing how a person behaves when they're sober isn't enough.

The Master's Checklist:

Masters choose their wingmen (and wingwomen) with great care. Wingmen meet the following criteria

- **Coolheaded**

- **Not a troublemaker**

- **Funny—but not an asshole**

- **Alert**

- **Intuitive: Can sniff out trouble**

"You have to drink with them to truly know how they'll perform in the co-pilot's seat," Drunk Tzu said. "Alcohol can turn the most decent people into flaming hemorrhoids of humanity."

Passengers can even be assets for the master—if properly trained. A trained wingman will help serve as an extra set of eyes to help them spot cops, without rubber-necking and check for areas of potential threats. They can watch while the master concentrates on the road. When they see a cruiser, or an unmarked car, they issue the universal command of "cop!"

Masters also impart lessons on how to identify bogies to their wingman.

"I took my friend out looking for cops one night, just to show them how a cop car looks at night and how to adjust the rear view mirror to lessen the headlight glare, which offers a better view of the bubble lights," Mark D. said.

The wingman is also an alert navigator, keeping track of directions and watching for signs and unexpected traffic hazards when the driver is concerned with keeping the car on the road, according to Mark D.

Use Humor

A wingman with a good sense of humor can help diffuse situations with police, as well. Mark D., who has served as a wingman on numerous missions, gave an example from his own experiences.

"A few years back, I was traveling with my friend, lets call him 'Dave,' when he was pulled over by a state trooper during what cops term a 'roving patrol,'" Mark D. narrated. "The trooper asked him to perform a few sobriety tests. The first he aced. Then the trooper asked Dave to recite his A-B-C's. Immediately, my friend said A… B…. D."

"I immediately shouted, 'Holy shit, Dave. He gave you the first three letters!!!!' " Mark D. continued. "The trooper and Dave laughed so hard that he told us just to go straight home and he wouldn't say a word. He was still smiling when we left."

Mark D. cautioned that the humor must be self-deprecating; in other words, the driver or the wingman should make fun of themselves—not the cop.

"Otherwise, the cop is just going to think you're a smart ass," Mark D. said. "Not what you want."

Chapter 7: The Ultimate Test and the Master's Toolbox

Masters believe that the preparations, the training, and the insights obviously give them an advantage over most motorists who choose to indulge in an alcoholic beverage. But they don't believe it makes them immune. The master must dig deep into his or her tool box of techniques and tricks, when confronting the "ultimate test" on the road.

Evasive Maneuvering

For the casual driver, evasive maneuvering is the first, and sometimes only line of defense; for the master, this is one of the last layers of protection. It's still important, but; the master relies almost as heavily on the preparation and planning stages as he or she does on the need to out-maneuver the cop on the highway.

> *"After all, that's their (the cops) home turf," Mark D. said. "Unless you're a truck driver or road kill, nobody spends more time on the road."*

"After all, that's their home turf," Mark D. said. "Unless you're a truck driver or road kill, nobody spends more time on the road."

One of the first things a master learns is how to recognize the conditions when evasive maneuvering is necessary—and when to employ it.

This, of course, starts with police identification, masters say. During daytime hours, identifying police cruisers is easy—at night, it's an art unto itself.

The 70-30 Rule

Day, or night, Mark D. uses the "70-30 rule." He watches the road in front of him and scans for cops 70 percent of the time and checks his rear view mirror for the law 30 percent of the time. Mark D. said he has familiarized himself with the makes and models of police cruisers—local and state, marked an unmarked. For instance, he has also learned that unmarked cruisers in his state are usually ominous-looking Crown Victorias. Mark D. studies headlight configurations of these models so he can easily identify these vehicles no matter which way the police are coming—approaching in the opposite lane, or sneaking up behind him.

If a cop appears, that doesn't necessarily make Mark D. initiate evasive maneuvering techniques. In fact, Mark D. said that the cop, just like the rattlesnake, may take any sudden movement as a provocation: he'll coil and strike.

Mark D. said if a cop is approaching him in the opposite lane, he avoids eye contact with the officer and drives naturally, then waits for signs that this cop has "coiled."

For instance, after the cop passes, Mark D. checks his rearview mirror. If he sees brake lights, Mark D. assumes the cop is attempting to reverse directions to get on his tail and automatically. Mark D. starts evasive manuevering.

"Another sign is that the cop will rapidly pull out of his parking space," Mark said.

Mark D. said he resists the urge to either speed up or immediately drop his speed; nor will he take sudden turns—not yet, at least.

> **The Master's Facts:**
>
> Cops are often trained to take the first right if they lose sight of a suspect in a vehicle. That's the theory of least resistance. The master attempts to find the first left… and takes that.

"Not only does this confirm the cop's suspicions," Mark said. "It gives him probable cause to pull you over."

Mark D. stays calm. Since cops are trained to take the nearest right if they lose sight of the suspect, Mark D. immediately takes the first possible left.

"This may seem counter-intuitive; after all the right turn represents the path of least resistance," Mark D. said. "But that's just what the cops are thinking."

Once he hits the turn, Mark D. will speed up and attempt to take unexpected routes. He then attempts to backtrack and continue on his mission.

"Since my mission has been compromised, I will immediately go to home base," Mark D. said. "No more bar hopping. I call it an evening."

Bandit at Six O'clock!

If evasive maneuvering does not work, or if a cop has unexpectedly appeared on their tail, masters continue to employ evasive maneuvering techniques—albeit raised another notch.

Masters indicate that the driver must first relax.

"Cops can detect fear by the way someone drives almost as easy as they can smell liquored-up breath," Drunk Tzu said.

Drunk Tzu said he maintains the course and does not continually check the cop in his rear view mirror. A glance is okay—even normal, Drunk Tzu said, but too many looks will tip off his suspicion. If someone is driving with Drunk Tzu, he advises them to not look around—no redneck rubbernecking—and to act normally.

He also sits back in his seat—police often note that drunk drivers creep up close to their steering wheel and peer out of the windshield like a blind man test driving a new car. Another tell-tale sign of drunk driving is the tendency for drivers to hug the middle line, Drunk Tzu said. By relaxing, settling into the seat and guiding the car along the middle of the lane, the driver will diminish some of these warning signs, Drunk Tzu said.

(According to Drunk Tzu, these driving techniques should be applied all the time, regardless of whether or not the driver is being followed by the police.)

Of course, the natural reaction for someone being followed by a cop is to pull over. Another common mistake is to swing into a driveway, even if it isn't the motorist's driveway, just to get out of the cop's way. Those are some very bad ideas, Drunk Tzu indicated.

"This only forces the cop to make an immediate decision: to let you go, or to act on his suspicions, hit the lights and bust you," Drunk Tzu said. "The chances are too great that he'll do the latter."

"Hopefully, he'll lose interest and drop off your tail,' Drunk Tzu said. "Or maybe another call will come in for a suspected drunk driver. Damn them drunk drivers."

Disabled Vehicle

If a vehicle breaks down or is disabled in any fashion, masters immediately consider the mission compromised, get the car to the side of the road, and then seek other forms of transportation—including the old shoe leather express. Once in a safe locale, they call for a tow truck, or they wait a full twelve hours to undertake their own recovery mission.

The reason is simple, according to Mary C.—disabled vehicles attract police. She offers one incident that served to help cement this rule as one of her bedrock principles of DUI Avoidance.

"My friend and her husband were out one night and got a flat," Mary C. said. "They were only a mile or so from their house, so he walked her home and went back to change the tire. When he returned, the police were waiting. Maybe they smelled alcohol, or maybe they were just playing the odds that most guys out on Saturday night in a Trans Am are drunk; but for whatever reason, they tested him for drunk driving and took him in."

"He would have never got busted if he would have just stayed at home," Mary C. said. "Now that's a hard lesson to learn."

"If it's broke, don't fix it—at least until after breakfast," Mary C. said. "That's my rule."

Chapter 8: Cultivating the Bond

If, despite the best efforts at evasive maneuvering, the cop hits the lights and signals for the driver to pull over, the master never loses faith—and maintains his or her cool.

"Everything I've done up to this point, all the planning and the preparation, can still stack the deck in my favor," Kevin D. said. "It may be hard to believe, but at this point, I am confident I am going to pull away scott-free."

Kevin D., who said he has been pulled over at least seven times in various stages of inebriation, goes through the following procedure.

If the radio is on, he turns it off. He also turns off the engine.

Any evidence, or evidence that might suggest drinking, are quickly "spirited" away into the designated spot.

Kevin keeps his information paperclipped together in the glove compartment.

He pulls this out and keeps them on his lap, waiting for the cop to advance.

While waiting, he takes care of his breath. This master keeps a range of breath-freshening products—gum, peanut butter candy, sweet drops, and cough drops —on hand and at the ready for easy access. (Kevin drops some Visine in his eyes each time he leaves a bar.)

Limiting Exposure, Establishing the Bond

Keeping his paper work in order helps the master accomplish a few things, Kevin D. said, it limits his exposure time, creates a favorable impression, and lays the groundwork to bond with the cop.

> **The Master's Facts:**
> When masters are pulled over, they hope that each step they have taken up to that point will lead to the payoff—getting off Scott-free. They aim to limit the exposure time with the cop and allay any suspicion that may turn a routine stop into a DUI arrest.

According to Kevin, the exposure time is the period when the cop has the ability to observe the driver up close and personal.

"When he gets to that window, he's gonna be looking at you real close," Kevin D. said. "When you have everything ready as soon as he appears at your window, this is going to limit the time the cop has to give you the lab rat treatment."

Kevin D. reported that the polite routine works best—as long as it isn't overplayed.

"I don't go for too much of the 'yes-officer, no-officer' crap, I just call them sir, and don't overuse the officer bit," Kevin D. said. "The police are people, too, and I assume they hate a suck-ass just as much as I do."

If the officers happened to search the car, Kevin D. said he would allow them.

"I have never had the cops want to search my car. If they wanted to I would let them," Kevin D. said. "If they're lucky, the most they would find is a couple of empties."

"They won't be getting in the trunk, though," he added. "I seem to have lost the key."

Favorable impression

Masters consider other preparations to help foster a favorable impression, according to Albert P.

A neat car and a neat appearance certainly help, he said. Albert P. also makes sure his photo ID represents a clean-cut, upstanding individual.

"I shaved off my Fu-manchu moustache forty minutes before I went to take this picture," Albert said as he hands over his driver's license showing a clean-shaven, short-haired, middle-aged man. "I look like I'm a narc, don't I."

Albert P., who served in the Marines back in the 80s, keeps a "Semper Fi" sticker on his back window. Since cops have the same human tendency to resist turning on their own, he believes this helps him "cultivate a bond" that is hard to break.

"Not all cops are assholes, some can be downright good people," Albert P. said. "My Semper FI sticker might be able to make a connection with an ex-Marine cop. Even, if a cop is an Army vet, the insignia could still give us a chance to connect on some level, even if it's him teasing me about being a jarhead."

Albert P. said that only real veterans should use this technique.

He said that if someone doesn't have military experience, and the police were to investigate further, the driver's answers may not jibe with the cop's experience.

"Or, he may find out through some other means: He could isolate and talk to the loudmouth

> *"You're probably also looking at a dozen or so related charges—reckless driving, resisting arrest, speeding, etc—all because you broke the bond," Albert P. said. "The military card is not the only one to be played to help cultivate a bond between you and the officer, so the risks outweigh the rewards."*

driving with you and make him spill his guts," Albert P. said. "Or, he could even check your records, if he's feeling pricky enough."

If this happens, according to Albert P., the bond would be permanently broken and DUI is almost assured.

"You're probably also looking at a dozen or so related charges— reckless driving, resisting arrest, speeding, etc—all because you broke the bond," Albert P. said. "The military card is not the only one to be played to help cultivate a bond between you and the officer, so the risks outweigh the rewards."

Albert P.'s vehicle has no other decals and no novelty items inside. Once again, he said this helps him facilitate a favorable impression.

As stressed by other masters, just as some car decorations can help, others can create an almost instant negative relationship between the cop and the driver, Kevin D. indicated.

"Rock and rap stickers and decals sporting liberal slogans are like throwing on a red coat while you're walking through the bull stall—bound to get you just the attention you don't want," Kevin D. said. "I doubt an "Ice-T" or "Marilyn Manson" sticker will win you any points."

Another no-no, is to look too rich, Albert P. said. He not only avoids high end cars, he always dresses conservatively when he ventures out under the influence, like the "common man."

"There's a fine line between hick and working class, but most cops consider themselves blue collar," Albert P. said. "So should you."

"A cop with a severe case of class envy, may just be itching to take get at 'daddy's' money, by fining the shit out of you," Albert P. added.

Interacting

Heretofore, almost all of the favorable impression has been created without ever speaking a word, Chuck R. pointed out. Vocal interaction with the cop must now reinforce this impression, he continued. Chuck R. has compiled a list of the "Three B's" of cop-drunk driver communication.

Be Cooperative

First, the driver must be cooperative, according to Chuck R.. This means utilizing a friendly, open channel of communication, that Kevin D. stressed. It also means the driver never loses his temper—even if it means he or she has to settle for a bull shit, yet lesser, charge such as speeding or reckless driving.

"Be happy to be considered a reckless driver, instead of a drunk driver," Chuck R. said. "There ain't an organization called Mothers Against Reckless Drivers, is there?"

Be in Control

Even an innocent driver pulled over for a minor infraction will exhibit signs of nervousness—that's natural—but an officer will look for undue signs of fear and, especially, guilt. Therefore, remaining in control alleviates some of these suspicions.

Eyes should be fixed, nervous twitches should be minimized, and the voice should sound confident, Chuck R. emphasized.

"Taking some deep breathes as the cop approaches may help," Chuck R. added.

(As mentioned before, keeping the car neat, and all documents in order, help reinforce the perception that the motorist is in control, Chuck R said. Plus, it makes the driver feel more confident, since he or she is not flustered looking for papers and cards.)

Be Concise

Communication with the cop should be kept to short, precise answers.

Chuck R. resists the urge to ramble on. He sticks to the parameters of his story—a well-rehearsed excuse that he drew up long before the mission—and refuses to be drawn into other conversations.

"Resist the urge to be a smart ass. A single smart ass answer can not only signal the end of a beautiful night, but also the end of a DUI-free driving record," Chuck R. said.

For instance, according to Chuck R., never say:

The Master's Checklist:

Just some excuses that just won't cut it, according to the masters:

- I'm sorry I missed that stop sign. I was just too drunk to see it.

- Can you hold my beer while I get my registration out of the glove compartment?

- I thought there were physical fitness standards for cops?

- I'm sorry I missed that stop sign. I was just too drunk to see it.

- Can you hold my beer while I get my registration out of the glove compartment?

- I didn't catch your name… are you Andy or Barney?

- I thought there were physical fitness standards for cops?

- When the Officer said "Gee son, Your eyes look red, have you been drinking?" You shouldn't respond with, "Gee Officer, our eyes look glazed, have you been eating donuts?"

- Did anyone tell you that you look like Sipowitz, except a little uglier.

"If you want to develop a stand-up routine, that's fine," Chuck R. said. "Now's not the time for rehearsals, though."

Chapter 9: Is it ever too late?

Is it too late, if the cop places the cuffs on you and reads you your rights? Many drunk drivers assume so, but the masters disagree.

"It ain't over until the fat drunk sings," Drunk Tzu said.

"Most people get mad at the cop," Drunk Tzu said, "This is not helpful. It is amazing that people think that calling their arresting office a 'fat, son of a bitch' would be beneficial to their cause."

Masters never give up talking their way out the situation. They continually probe the cop for areas of weakness—sympathies that they can exploit including kids, mutual interests, shared experiences, anything. The one behavior that will ensure a DUI is the ever-escalating temper.

"Most people get mad at the cop," Drunk Tzu said, "This is not helpful. It is amazing that people think that calling their arresting office a 'fat, son of a bitch' would be beneficial to their cause."

Drunk Tzu said that the cop will probably not reply, "You know, I guess you're right; I could stand to drop a little weight and my mom often exhibited domineering tendencies. Here let me get you out of those cuffs."

Case in Point

Kevin D. offered an example from his own past that illustrates how he plucked victory from the certain jaws of defeat.

"I was in the cuffs, man," Kevin D. said. "I put my vehicle in a ditch and the cops—there were two of them— thought they smelled booze, so I was on my way to the hospital for the blood test."

"I had a few beers," Kevin D. admitted. "But I figured I was real close to the legal limit, or a little over, so my goal was to delay the test as much as possible."

Keep Your Cool Shall be the Whole of the Law

Option one, according to Kevin D., was to kick, scream, and generally act like an imbecile. Kevin D, however, recognizes that keeping cool is the whole of the law for a master in such a situation.

"That strategy would, one: reinforce the cops' suspicions that I was drunk, and two: make them drive faster to the hospital," Kevin D. said.

Instead, Kevin D. chose to talk intelligently and politely. He probed the two officers with questions.

"I mentioned that my father was in Vietnam." Kevin D. said. "As soon as I said that, the officer in the passenger seat, who was obviously the senior of the two cops, told the cop driving to pull over."

Kevin D. added, "I was just hoping he wasn't going to shoot me. I couldn't figure out what I said."

As the cruiser engine idled, the officer began to question Kevin D. about his father's service in Vietnam. He explained that his father fought for the 1st Infantry Division (the Big Red One) in Nam between 1967 and 1968, a fact that seemed to peak the interest of the officer.

"Turns out that the cop was in Vietnam in 1968 and was assigned to the same division," Kevin D. said. "They were apparently at the same base at the same time—though they never met, it seemed."

The cop exited the cruiser and tugged open the door to the back seat. He helped Kevin D. stand up and turned him around. He took off the cuffs.

"He pointed to a phone booth at a nearby shopping center, and said, 'you call the tow truck from there,' " Kevin D. said. "Then he told me, 'It's about a mile back to your car, by the time you walk back there, I'm betting the alcohol from those two beers will burn out of your system. I'm also betting you're going to drive that car straight back home and stay off the road for the rest of the day, right?' "

"I did exactly what the man said," Kevin D. said. "That was the closest call I ever had."

D.U.Cry

Mary C. is prepared to unleash the waterworks as a final resort.

"For a female, it's okay to bawl like they're taking bamboo splints from your fingernails, or they're taking the Oxygen Channel off your cable service," Mary C. said.

However, she cautions males not to use the technique.

"By the way, crying hysterically isn't a good look on a man," Mary C. said with a laugh. "Sorry guys."

Know the Law

Knowing a good lawyer is not good enough for most masters who insist that obtaining a thorough knowledge of state laws and their loopholes is a necessity.

For example, laws concerning blood, breathalyzer, and sobriety field tests vary from state to state. In the states where these tests are voluntary, masters would recommend immediately refusing to take the test because accepting punishment for a lesser crime is better than gambling that they can beat the test.

"My game plan is to tell them I will submit to a test at the hospital to buy time and to keep the lines of communication open with the cop." Chuck R. said. "I can always change my mind at the hospital."

Much of this information can be obtained online, or through interviews from those arrested for DUI.

"I'll even talk to a cop," Chuck R. said. "I guess I should add that I would talk to them when I was sober."

Already Have a DUI?

None of the masters who were interviewed had received a DUI, obviously. They stated that prior DUI drivers make huge targets.

First, the pull-over will resurrect immediate suspicions when the cop checks the driver's record.

"Though I have been pulled over four times, I have been let go four times," Drunk Tzu said. "All because my record is clean. If I would have been caught early on, I would have been nailed numerous times."

Secondly, some police have a record of prior offenders and will pull them over routinely. States may begin to make this somewhat unethical approach a legal reality by creating a database of license plate numbers and allowing police to randomly pull over drivers who show up on this list.

Also, repeat offenders may have much deeper problems with alcohol than the casual drinker, Drunk Tzu believed, and this makes them a rich source of costs and fines for the police.

"Once you're in the system, the man wants you to stay and pay," Drunk Tzu said. "Avoiding the first DUI is the best step, but casual drinkers with a DUI on their records have to be extremely careful."

www.ingramcontent.com/pod-product-compliance
Lightning Source LLC
Chambersburg PA
CBHW022107170526
45157CB00004B/1523